Un~~stuck~~
WORKBOOK

HOW TO TALK TO
HUMANS
& *GET THEM TO RESPOND*
TO YOU

Sarah Harnisch
Young Living Diamond

Book 2 of 3 in the Gameplan Trilogy

CONTENTS

Edited by Debbie Knox Wheeler

Layout and cover art by Cory Rucker

THE UNSTUCK COMPREHENSIVE STRATEGY WORKBOOK

INTRODUCTION

What?? There is homework for the introduction? Yes. It's a tough assignment. Every single one of these pages is meant to help you process and work through your Young Living business and to become relatable, so you draw others in. Part of that is processing the road we've already been on. You will be a stronger leader if you find a way to integrate, not just your gifts and talents, but also your pain, your mistakes, and your journey into your business story.

When we were at the Young Living International Grand Convention in Utah in 2019, we were told to share our stories. I gave you some of my darkest dirt in this chapter. While I was going through it, I thought going that my life had no meaning; that my story could not benefit or bless anyone.

I was wrong.

We're going to practice writing out our oils stories later on in this workbook. That's not the purpose of the assignment today. Today I want you to think through your dark places. Take me to the rough spots where you wanted to give up. Share your road with me as if we were sitting on the couch across from one another. Then, I want you to think about who that story may bless. Who may be able to relate to it? For me, it's busy moms, moms of special needs kids, overwhelmed women, women who are exhausted at work (who feel unappreciated), women who have not found their place of rest, those battling depression, anxiety, fear; and if I can say it openly, suicide. That's where I can speak into others with my journey.

Why do I have you penning something so deep right at the get-go? It's who you are, even if it's embarrassing or dark. The purpose of this book is to help you connect with others. To do that, you have to know what your places of connecting are. You have to know who YOU are. What do you love? Who do you love? How do you spend your time? What are you passionate about? What do you do for income? What makes you you? What things inside you can be used as a talking point to draw others closer?

Assignment 1:

Tell me one of the toughest moments of your life.

_____

_____

_____

_____

_____

_____

_____

_____

_____

_____

_____

Assignment 2:

Tell me some of the things that make you unique. What things can you use as talking points to connect with people? For me, I worked in the food industry for many years (11 different jobs) before I started my first radio job. I connect well with people in retail, waitressing, or anyone making someone a sandwich or delivering a pizza. For hobbies, I love running, gardening, writing, singing, cleaning and organizing (ok, that's weird; maybe that's not a point of connecting to people!). I love kids. I have 5 of them, and two grandkids. I love loud music and time away with my husband. I love laughing really, really hard. I love reading non-fiction prolifically, and outlining and researching all I come across. I geek out over clean living. I love the newsroom and writing against a clock. I love the sun on my face. These are some of the places I can connect with people. Before we study how to connect with others, learn what your own talking points are. It will give you a doorway for the types of people to look for in stores and restaurants, and out and about.

What makes you unique?

_____

_____

_____

_____

_____

_____

_____

_____

_____

_____

_____

_____

Assignment 3:

When I am in a store, I deliberately look around to seek out people that may be like-minded. I always have an eye out for those that may be sick. I am always listening, looking, and trying to connect. I don't connect to be creepy. I connect to love and help other people. Based on the stories above, what types of people can you be on the lookout for? In my case, it would be moms, people checking out healthier options in stores (or starting down an essential oils aisle), people with running gear in their carts, someone humming next to me, or someone with a stack of books in their arms. These are some people that would catch my attention, because we're engaged in the same things, and it won't be hard to strike up a conversation.

Who catches your attention? Likewise, who would connect with you?

_____

If you know you, you start to know them. You're not spending time writing all of this out to be a better you, or to learn to talk about you more. It's the start of an exercise to begin to know those around you more. Ask a leading question that connects you with the person near you because you have things in common. Let this page be a kickoff to a conversation starter. Then stay silent and listen to their needs. Listening and offering a suggestion is how you get your business off the ground.

My name is

_____

And I am a Young Living Royal Crown Diamond.

CHAPTER 1

WHY YOUNG LIVING IS THE BEST JOB IN THE WORLD (AND WHY YOU SHOULD GO FOR IT)

Make a list of some of the perks of Young Living. Side by side, write down if you have those perks at your same job. For example...

Young Living   My Job

Get to set my own work hours   Work 9-5, with some 50-hour weeks

I want you to see, side by side, the pros of this business and where it goes. If you haven't thought it through very closely, this will give you a great perspective on why this truly is the best job in the world—even if you love what you're doing.

Young Living   My Job

_____   _____

_____   _____

_____   _____

_____   _____

_____   _____

_____   _____

_____   _____

_____   _____

_____   _____

_____   _____

One of my favorite graphics in the book is the Diamond Rising average monthly income graphic. I remember seeing this right after I'd gotten my first Young Living check after teaching one class. That check was half of my weekly pay as a news anchor, even though I'd only "worked" my Young Living business for about two hours for that one class. What is your monthly budget?

What income on that chart would give you a leg up?
Write the rank and income here: _____

What income on that chart would truly change the way you live?

_____

Now we're going to do something a bit weird, but it's part of vision casting. I want you to write out your monthly budget as if you were debt free. My monthly budget doesn't include a mortgage, credit card debt, or student loan debts. It does include things like food, utilities, travel to see my team, and speak, and philanthropy. My goal when I started Young Living was to live on 10-percent of my income and tithe 90-percent—the reverse tithe.

What does your budget look like with no debt, on a Royal Crown Diamond's monthly average salary of above $144,551? How would you use that check if it came every single month for the rest of your life? Write down your Royal Crown Diamond "budget" below:

My Royal Crown Diamond Monthly Budget

_____   _____

_____   _____

_____   _____

_____   _____

_____   _____

_____   _____

_____   _____

_____   _____

_____   _____

_____   _____

_____   _____

I know you may not be doing this for the income. As a matter of fact, I can't think of a single business builder where that is their only objective. However, it's completely true that this business changes lives forever financially. 50-percent of all marriages end in divorce; and the number one reason is finances. It's fighting over where the cash from your 9 to 5 will go. It's a raw fact that having an increased income, whether that's your motivation or not, will change many things for the better: the health of the relationships around you, stress levels, and the ability to give generously (which activates a part of the brain that also makes you feel joyful and content). I love drawing out my monthly budget. I realized that as a Royal, most of the things on my current budget would be gone in one or two month's pay. That pressure valve relief makes this just one more reason why Young Living is worth the fight.

Every month that you have a no-show class, a dissident leader, or are frustrated over a shipping issue, or an email, or a post you see online, or a few rough words... look back at your long-term goals. Laying this thing down brick by brick, no matter how many rough days there are, is still worth the fight.

CHAPTER 2

NO ONE IS LISTENING

Let's do some fill in the blanks, because the numbers in this chapter are important.

How many new Diamonds were there in November 2017? _____

How many new Diamonds were there in all of 2016? _____

How many new Diamonds were there in all of 2017? _____

How many Silvers, Golds, and Platinums were there in 2016? _____

How many Silvers, Golds, and Platinums were there in 2017? _____

What increase is that? _____

How many no-show classes has my sister Rachael had? _____

The biggest obstacle on your way to Diamond is _____

The average Diamond hits rank in _____ years

Make up a list of the desires of your heart! Tell me your biggest dreams below. Where do you want this thing to go??

_____

_____

_____

_____

_____

_____

_____

_____

_____

Let's make this chapter an action step. I ended it by telling you to PLAY.

Get out your reference guide. Get out your catalogue. Pick five oils you don't have and research them. What do they do? What would you need them for? Let's run YOU through an aromatherapy funnel. It's going to be really hard for you to train people when you've never played. Have you allowed yourself time to PLAY? To research? To learn new things, or are you in survival mode?

I chicken scratched my oils research into my first catalogue. You can do that, or you can write some things you want to try below. Research five oils. Then, I want you to make your own Essential Rewards wish list at 300pv for three months. What are all the things you're dying to try? Let's write them out together.

GATHER YOUR STORY: TESTIMONY GATHERING 101

Let me be bold here and tell you what I did with my first wish list. I made a list of my top three health ailments. Then, I got out my reference guide and started to play, right after I got my kit. Issue one was my adrenals. I was TIRED. I drank 2 bottles of NingXia in 2 weeks, then started on some Super B and Nutmeg topically over my adrenal glands. It was a game changer for me personally!

Issue 2 was my lymph nodes. They kept swelling! In fact, I'd done lymph tinctures and dry brushing, trampoline jumping, and they'd been swollen for seven solid months (8-12 pea-sized lymph nodes under each arm, with golf-ball sized nodes occasionally). When I looked it up in the reference guide, it suggested Grapefruit oil. Even on a ministry salary, I could afford that! I got it and tried it. The third time, it did this:

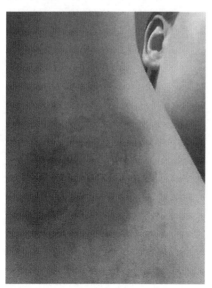 

Hey, it's not every day you get to see an author's ARMPITS in a workbook! This is special! Also incredibly embarrassing! I would never have had this story if I hadn't played around.

I played around a third time in the first week I had my kit. I also struggle with a lot of swelling during my cycles. It's irritating. I look like the stay-puff marshmallow. When I researched that online, it suggested Copaiba oil. This was my before and after, as part of my personal story. It happened in two hours.

I would never have had these stories if I hadn't played around. I am not a doctor, and I never will be. I am a mom. I can't diagnose things. The photos above aren't serious issues. However, for me, they were nuisances. By playing with my reference guide and playing with the oils, I now had stories I could share.

Start with the commitment to play. That will generate excitement and stories, which leads to passion. With passion, people will listen. They will follow hope. Hope is generated when you play.

Oil 1: _____

Who needs it in my family: _____

_____

What that oil does: _____

_____

_____

_____

_____

_____

_____

Oil 2: _____

Who needs it in my family: _____

_____

What that oil does: _____

_____

_____

_____

_____

_____

Oil 3: _____

Who needs it in my family: _____

_____

What that oil does: _____

_____

_____

_____

_____

_____

Oil 4: _____

Who needs it in my family: _____

_____

What that oil does: _____

_____

_____

_____

_____

_____

_____

Oil 5: _____

Who needs it in my family: _____

_____

What that oil does: _____

_____

_____

_____

_____

_____

_____

_____

My 3-Month Essential Rewards Wish List

Month 1: (write down the item number so it's easy for you to add to your cart later!)

Month 2:

Month 3:

CHAPTER 3

THE STATE OF STUCK

What does Proverbs 18:21 say? _____

_____

Make a list of everything you believe about your business RIGHT now. Then I want you to write the reciprocal of that. Put them side by side. Every morning your head is in the gutter, get this list out and read the positive side only. This IS worth fighting for. YOU are worth fighting for.

I LOVE this fact in Unstuck! If a room were filled with _____ people, only _____ would have a starter kit, and _____ would not. SATURATION IS A MYTH.

My strategy when I first start to build is to sign my _____immediately.

You were born to _____.

Focus on this one single thing: _____.

Your doubt is disassembling _____.

CHAPTER 4

MOJO METHOD 1: UTILIZE YOUR FORGOTTEN WARM MARKET

Mojo sets the tone _____

When you believe, it's a straight track to _____.

All you have to do is _____.

Let's put this mojo method to action. Make a list of EVERY person you know below. Pull some ideas on where to get the list from this chapter. Then put pencil to paper and start writing down names. Those are the people you start with. Need a quick place to start? Open your cell phone contacts list. You can do it!

MY WARM MARKET

_____   _____

_____   _____

_____   _____

_____   _____

_____   _____

_____   _____

_____   _____

CHAPTER 5

MOJO METHOD 2: PURPLE BAGS

This chapter is easy to do. Make a bag and hand it out!

If you're on a tight budget, burn the 101 cd off my website for free (you can get cheap cd's at Sam's Club or Walmart). Print off the cover sheet and the "Steps to Purchase Your Starter Kit Sheet" sheet from my website for free. Print the *Fearless* calendar for free. Start from that place.

What do I put in my bags? I go all out.

I do:

☐ A cover sheet.

☐ A photo of the starter kit (I love the discoverlsp.com fliers).

☐ A 101 cd or a Toxin Free Life cd.

☐ *Fearless.*

☐ The *Fearless* calendar (oilabilityteam.com/fearless).

☐ The mini: *Your Gameplan: Build A Life Beyond Survival Mode.*

☐ Instructions on how to order (free at oilabilityteam.com/follow-up-bags/) .

☐ My business card with my contact info.

☐ Occasionally a sample of Young Living product like Cool Azul pain cream or Thieves Whitening toothpaste, or Thieves cough drops.

Then I ALWAYS collect their contact info.

Mojo challenge 2: make up five of these bags with whatever contents you want; and make it a point to hand them to perfect strangers this week. Then, collect their contact info, even if it's just a Facebook friending.

CHAPTER 6

MOJO METHOD 3: VENDOR EVENTS

What are the seven bulletpoints you can begin right now to prepare for a vendor event?

_____

_____

_____

_____

_____

What are the obstacles with a vendor event?

_____

_____

_____

_____

_____

You have permission to skip to the vendor events chapter and read ahead in the book!

What are some things you're going to try with your event?

_____

_____

_____

_____

_____

Now start scheduling a few events! Get your first three booked and write them down here:

_____

_____

_____

_____

_____

CHAPTER 7

MOJO METHOD 4:
FRIENDS OF FRIENDS

Mojo Method 4: Friends of Friends

I think one of the most important things you can do when you sign someone

is to _____

_____

Set their first class up _____

I believe in empowering _____

Make it your personal goal to sign your circle. Then sign their circle. Pick at least five family members and love on them (just like you did in the earlier chapter when you pulled out your reference guide and looked things up for yourself. Do that same action with them and show them how to research.) Then, love on your family's family members.

Check each box when you have picked five people close to you (it may be a friend, family, or an acquaintance). Then commit to getting them fired up on oils. Train them to research and label read, to look for poison in their home, and look things up. Once they have their "WOW" moment, tap into their friend circles, and sign their circle.

Once they are on ER, circle the box. If you complete this one exercise, and each of these people get on ER, you'll have 40 people on your team. That's almost halfway to Silver, simply by signing circles.

Friend 1: ☐ Circle signed and on ER: ☐ ☐ ☐ ☐ ☐ ☐ ☐ ☐ ☐ ☐

Friend 2: ☐ Circle signed and on ER: ☐ ☐ ☐ ☐ ☐ ☐ ☐ ☐ ☐ ☐

Friend 3: ☐ Circle signed and on ER: ☐ ☐ ☐ ☐ ☐ ☐ ☐ ☐ ☐ ☐

Friend 4: ☐ Circle signed and on ER: ☐ ☐ ☐ ☐ ☐ ☐ ☐ ☐ ☐ ☐

Friend 5: ☐ Circle signed and on ER: ☐ ☐ ☐ ☐ ☐ ☐ ☐ ☐ ☐ ☐

Once you hit this goal, I like to try to sign 10 people under each friend and get them on Essential Rewards. That one action would be enough for them to get their Essential Rewards order for free. That's thinking about them, not you. It doesn't matter if they never do the business. You have grown your OGV by signing circles, so it will bless you. Even more importantly, you have given them oils for a lifetime for their family. Goal 2, advanced strategy, would be to take those that pop and build them to the Rising Star structure. Get seven legs to 300 OGV so they see it in their check. Those that don't pop... don't stress about it. Move on to the next circle. Those that don't build the business can still order Thieves at no cost with their check! That's what this is all about: getting oils into every home in the world.

CHAPTER 8

IF ALL YOUR MOJO METHODS FAIL

Fill in the blank:

Talking to your friends and family can be incredibly frustrating. If they are the

only voices you hear on this journey, _____

Some of my closest family members _____

Write down your personal fact sheet of why you oil!

You need a list of quick responses when people ask you, "why network marketing?", "why essential oils?", and "why Young Living?". One of my favorite responses to, "why network marketing?" is Pat Petrini's, "I Still Think It's a Pyramid Scheme" on YouTube. Bulletpoint these answers out so you can respond swiftly and confidently when people ask. For most, it's just education. If you educate, they understand, and in many cases will support you.

Why network marketing, for you? (Here is another great resource. We're in the top 10 in the world.) https://www.directsellingnews.com/global-100/

_____

_____

_____

_____

_____

_____

Why essential oils?

_____

_____

_____

_____

_____

_____

Why Young Living?

_____

_____

_____

_____

_____

_____

_____

What is the solution when someone says no?

_____

_____

_____

_____

Thoughts to consider:

98 percent of my business is not built on family and friends.

How big would your customer base be if you considered everyone outside your door?

What if no one was untouchable?

Family members can become distractions that will cost you everything.

Everyone could be on your team.

There are no barriers except the ones you place in front of yourself.

You must simply learn to talk to people you don't know.

Replace fear with confidence.

Replace doubt with hope.

Get outsideof your warm market.

Their freedom and your freedom are not tied together.

Dream as big as Gary Young.

Write a few thoughts out from this chapter below (things that hit you hard). Write down things that inspire you. When you're having a down day, and someone has told you no, return to Chapter 8 to pull your head from that place. No now is not no forever! Seed plant and move on.

My Thoughts:

CHAPTER 9

YOU ARE NOT FORGOTTEN

Words of encouragement: I am just a mom with a three-page script who shared from my couch and saw results (even when I didn't believe where it would go, even when my why was tiny). The Lord has taken my simplicity and disbelief, and has done amazing things with it. He can do it for you too. That soil is still wet on my own feet; and that journey is not yet finished.

Let's dissect exactly why you are frozen.

1) You have to get your head ready to run.

2) You need new ideas, because your ways of connecting have burned you out.

3) You need to learn how to fight fear most of all.

4) You need to know that your identity is not in what you do.

5) You need to learn the skill of connecting with strangers.

Fill this in:

There are many reasons why people_____

_____

Why do you think you are frozen? If you know where this goes, what it will do for your family financially, how it will impact your ability to give and help others, see the stats and know this is a way out for you... What holds you back? Be real, raw, and honest below.

Now I want you to write the opposite of every sentence you wrote above. Just take a moment and get that negativity out of your mind and focus on forward movement. This is a small exercise to show you that you're your own worst enemy! Write out word for word the polar opposite of what is above. Then KNOW that you have what it takes to do this business. Know it in your gut.

CHAPTER 10

WHY DON'T PEOPLE RESPOND TO YOU?

How do I personally get over rejection? It's simple really. I can answer that with one word: _____

How are you spending your time? Are you scheduling classes? Are you building relationships? Are you oiling people up? Are you teaching at least a class a week? If your nose is spent in aromatherapy books and helping oilers on other teams (that's generous, but does not take care of your family), or one hundred other activities. You're going to stay at your rank for a long time.

It's like saying you are hungry, and you want dinner; but you never open the fridge and make food. This business will not come to you. You have to work for it.

Write up a prayer for Abraham volume below, not because it's about you, but because it's about the impact you're going to have on thousands of families, like the stars in the sky. What words do you want spoken over them? What words do you want spoken over the leaders and the members that are not on your team yet? Pray over the right words to connect with them, before you have even met.

_____

_____

_____

_____

_____

_____

_____

_____

CHAPTER 11

TONGUE, HEAD, FEET

This is a powerful chapter. It undoes all excuse making. I want you to closely read through the paragraph that starts, "There are more than 450 Diamonds in Young Living right now..." and see what excuse I'm giving behind each sentence. Let me start with the first one and show you what I mean.

"There are Diamonds that started from extreme poverty and some that started with significant wealth."

"Excuse: I don't have enough money to get a kit/do the business/get on Essential Rewards."

Here is the next one:

There are Diamonds that began their organizations in large cities, and some that began in towns of 600.

Excuse: Everyone in my town has already heard about essential oils.

Now you take over! I'm going to give you several pages to tear apart in this chapter, because I want you to recognize an excuse when you see one. If you hear it coming out of your lips, ban it abruptly. You are bigger than these excuses! Don't allow them to come from you, or from any of your leaders. These are the types of sentences that delay a Diamondship. Diamonds find a way around the obstacle. They do not let the obstacle hold them back. If you don't have enough money for ER, sign your circle so you can afford it. Hold a yard sale to get the initial kit. Find a way around the mountain, without excuses.

Let's do some deep analysis of the most common excuses in Young Living. This section is worth the work! See through the words of what people are really saying, so you know how to respond.

All of the Diamonds did what three things to rank?

1)_____

2)_____

3)_____

You know what to do!

Drawing people in is easier than you think, because it does not depend on them. It depends on you.

My Experience Listening:

CHAPTER 12

THE ART OF LISTENING

You get them to listen by listening to them.

Write that out again: _____

You get people to listen by doing three things:

1)_____

2)_____

3)_____

STOP MAKING EVERY CONVERSATION ABOUT YOU.

Look for opportunities to serve them.

One on-fire oiler knows _____ by the time they are _____!

With one on-fire oiler, you could build _____ Silverships.

Write down the steps of how to listen to people:

1)_____

2)_____

3)_____

4)_____

5)_____

6)_____

The secret to relationships is _____.

What was your favorite "starter sentence" in this section, to open a conversation? _____

_____

_____

Now I want you to practice this. (WHAT THE WHAT??? THIS IS A WORKBOOK! THIS ISN'T A HANDS-ON TRADE SCHOOL!) Oh yes, it is!

Go out into a public place. Begin a random conversation with someone that appears to have a need for oils. It may be a place you're already familiar with, like a small group at church or a volunteering position. Run through steps 1, 2, and 3, and see where it leads you. Some of this is simply practicing the art of a new technique. Practice listening. Practice opening the conversation. Practice making it about them. Practice meeting needs. You'll do better than you think you would!

Write down your experience below:

CHAPTER 13

HOW TO COLLECT CONTACT INFORMATION

☐ Go check out the Scavenger Hunt video here: https://oilabilityteam. com/free-stuff/

What are some of the things you've already swapped out for Young Living that you no longer buy at the store? Write a brief list:

_____   _____

_____   _____

_____   _____

_____   _____

_____   _____

_____   _____

_____   _____

Those are your passion places! That's your heart, and the place where I'd start sharing. That's how you open the conversation with new people, using something off that list above. Then you close the conversation by saying, "I want to make sure you're ok. Is it ok if I friend you on Facebook?" (Or a similar sentence that feels comfortable to you.)

I gave you a list of sentences to collect their contact information. Pick one that resonates with you and write it on the lines below in a way that you would say it, using your voice. Everything I give you works when you make it yours: The 101 script (or any of the Core 4), the close, 30-second scripts to get people's attention at vendor events. It all has to be in your "speak."

Write down your leading sentence to capture contact info below:

_____

_____

You know I'm going to take this to the next level! Let's practice—for REALZ. Walk into an environment where you're unfamiliar with the people and collect someone's contact info. It can be a store, a restaurant, a parking lot, a sports field, or the SPCA (it doesn't matter where). If you are listening to their needs and offer a suggestion, most are willing to hand over their social media contact. If you're terrified to do this, do it more than once. It will become more comfortable, I promise! You have to keep one thing at the forefront of your mind: you are helping people. You are their difference. Don't even let the thought of what they think of you float across your brain. Focus on one thing: them. When you focus on you, you chicken out. When you focus on Them, you're making a difference in someone's life.

Check the boxes below each time you pick up a contact:

☐   ☐   ☐   ☐   ☐

What about closing your classes with confidence, in-person or online? Many times, it just comes down to having a script in your head so it rolls off your tongue. There are two short scripts at the end of this chapter to give you some confidence. Practice reading each and check the checkboxes below when you've read them aloud.

Script 1: ☐   ☐   ☐   ☐   ☐

Script 2: ☐   ☐   ☐   ☐   ☐

Copy these sentences word for word:

If I am not collecting contact information the first time I meet someone, either in a grocery store aisle, in a live class, or online, I am handing my paycheck to someone else. I have sowed seeds that someone else is going to harvest.

_____

_____

_____

_____

Lean on a script until you're comfortable. Then toss the script and go do you. The script is a set of training wheels to show you that YOU HAVE WHAT IT TAKES.

Remember one final thing: one sentence gets me almost everyone's contact information.

What is it?

CHAPTER 14

YOU ARE TELLING ME TO DO THINGS I HAVE ALREADY TRIED

What are some facts that "wowed" you at the start of this chapter?

_____

_____

_____

_____

_____ you make contact with is a potential oiler!

How Do You Think People Perceive You?

Check all that apply:

☐ Negative tongue

☐ Speak with sarcasm

☐ Speak with despair

☐ Have no fire, passion

☐ Exude weariness

☐ Posting divisive things on social media

☐ Indecisive

☐ Lack of confidence

☐ Facial expressions or body language don't match speech

What do you think you can do to rectify the way people perceive you? Do you think you need to be "fake" to pull that off, or can you find a genuine, authentic you that is still magnetic to the people around you?

_____

_____

_____

_____

Are you still stuck on this? Are you still having no kit sales? Let's do some training. Pick someone off this list and get a couple of their books, go watch a couple of their Youtube videos, or read a couple of articles they've posted online. Many of their resources are completely free and readily available. Write down any notes that hit you deeply. Get audiobooks of some of their work and listen to them during your down time; on your drive to work, when you're doing the dishes, etc... Don't waste opportunities to become a better network marketer.

Speakers that have inspired me:

Jim Rohn	Brendon Berchard	Dale Carnegie
Eric Worre	John Maxwell	Tony Robbins
Hal Alrod	Stephen Covey	Richard Bliss Brooke
Robert Kiyosaki	*Any* Young Living Diamond	

Train Your Brain Sessions

Pick someone above and listen to or read their content once a day for at least 15 minutes, for 30 straight days, to see if the way you're perceived by other people changes. Be an active listener and apply the tips you're hearing.

☐ ☐ ☐ ☐ ☐ ☐ ☐ ☐ ☐ ☐

☐ ☐ ☐ ☐ ☐ ☐ ☐ ☐ ☐ ☐

☐ ☐ ☐ ☐ ☐ ☐ ☐ ☐ ☐ ☐

These are of my favorite Young Living Diamond Resources:

☐ Jodie Meschuk and Sarah Lee's 3 Pillar Coaching (speakupbuttercup.com)

☐ Jim Bob Haggerton's Essential Oils Club (EOC) Facebook page

☐ Any book by Jim Bob Haggerton and Andy Jenkins (doctorjimbob.com)

☐ Oily App (cell phone app)

☐ Any book by Doctor Oli (doctoroli.com)

☐ Doc Oli's free yearly online Symposium with dozens of speakers is not to be missed (Google BioCode Academy)

- ☐ Melissa Poepping's Basi6 program (<u>melissapoepping.com/basi6</u>)
- ☐ Eric Walton's Downline Leadership program (<u>downlineleadership.com</u>)
- ☐ Vicki Opfer's Essential Sharing books (<u>discoverlsp.com</u>)
- ☐ Debra Raybern's "Road to Royal" books (<u>growinghealthyhomes.com</u>)
- ☐ Amanda Uribe's "Grow" series (<u>discoverlsp.com</u>)
- ☐ Jordan Schrandt's yearly Diamondbound event (<u>diamondboundevent.com</u>)
- ☐ Erin Rodgers has an entire store of goodness at <u>oilsupplystore.com</u>
- ☐ Joanna Malone's Level Up program (<u>joannamalone.com</u>)

These are good people that have the results you are looking for. When you finish *Unstuck*, don't stop training your brain! Your fire will come with the words spoken from these powerful leaders.

If you have not had results in a long time, focus only on _____

until you notice a change in your _____

If leadership training is slowing you down, _____

Sometimes we get so captivated by training systems, that we _____

CHAPTER 15

FEAR

If you put all of your time into training, and none of your time into implementing classes, you will not see growth in Young Living, or in any other network marketing business.

If I could give you one tip that I KNOW will help you rank this month, it would

be to _____

_____

Which things scare you in your business?

You know what I'm going to ask. I've already had you galivanting around practicing closes on people, collecting contact information..... This is the most action you've ever gotten from a workbook! But it works! You're practicing the actions that lead to direct business growth!

Face. Your. Fears.

You know exactly what you need to do. If you're afraid of talking to your closest friends, pick one and teach a 101. If you're afraid if speaking, go speak publicly. If you're afraid of rejection, go put yourself out there, even with the possibility of rejection. If you're afraid of Facebook Lives (yup, I went there...) go do a Facebook Live. If you're afraid of asking for contact info, go do it. If you're afraid of building relationships with strangers, build the relationships. If you're afraid of teaching because you don't feel that you know enough, teach. If you don't think you have enough of a story to share, go gather your story. (Yes, I just gave you permission to blow a ton of money on your Essential Rewards order!) What are you afraid of?? You have to face these things to get to freedom.

When you have done the thing that scares you in this business, I want you to do a coloring exercise below. Write inside the box, "I faced my fear." Then color it with a dozen colors and doodles. I am SO very proud of you. You just took ten steps forward in your business.

You have read my story of an identity crisis.

What are you placing your identity in? Is it work? Is it family? Is it being a mom or dad? Is it being a caregiver? Is it being a volunteer for something you're passionate about? Is your identity in a hobby? Who are you? When you know who you are, the decision of where you are going is much easier.

Live every day knowing _____

You are gathering experiences that you need to lead, and that your leaders need to rank. Tribulation is _____.

The practice comes _____

CHAPTER 16

THE KEY TO GROWTH

The key to confidence is PRACTICE. I'm never confident when I'm starting something new! It only rolls off my tongue if I've had a chance to do it a few times. The secret to your growth is sharing, in whatever way that looks like for you. When I say sharing, I'm talking about sharing the products that will lead to a 24 percent discount and a lifetime of Essential Rewards: the Core 4 starter kits. I've written scripts for each of them in the back of *Unstuck*.

I still read my own scripts, and it's been five years! I don't memorize anything. I just insert my own stories and make them mine. Each time I teach a class, it's just a little bit different based on the new things I've read, the new ways I've learned to oil, and the things others have imparted to me through their oils experiences. God gave us a playground when He gave us the plants!

Have YOU heard of the Core 4? Are you fully trained on the core products Young Living offers?

Have you listened to the 101 Oils, 102 Thieves, 103 NingXia, and 104 Savvy classes? Let's run you through the whole aromatherapy funnel while we're training business.

Over the next week, I want you to pick a lecture and do one of two things: either listen to the textable version of that class at oilabilityteam.com/Unstuck, or click on the professionally designed Powerpoints (and read the scripts that match them) in the back of this book. If you really want a leg up, do both. The textable class is a simple way of sharing. Snag the audio on my website for free, text the link to yourself, and listen to it on your cell phone as a podcast.

For the Powerpoint presentations and scripts, think about how you could read those yourself with confidence. Think about the stories you could tell between the lines. Those classes have been the key to my growth because they have led to starter kit sales.

Check off which classes you have attended below, as you drill yourself on the Core 4:

☐ 101 Oils textable class   ☐ 101 Oils Powerpoint + Scrip

☐ 102 Thieves textable class   ☐ 102 Thieves Powerpoint + Script

☐ 103 NingXia textable class   ☐ 103 NingXia Powerpoint + Script

☐ 104 Savvy textable class   ☐ 104 Savvy Powerpoint + Script

CHAPTER 17

HOW TO GET PEOPLE TO RESPOND 101

Let's go through the five tips to get someone's attention!

Tip 1: What would get your attention? Tell me below. If someone approached you with a bottle of oil, what would they have to do to get you try it?

_____

_____

_____

_____

Tip 2: Remember that the people you're speaking to are in total darkness when it comes to oils. Many have never tried them in their life. You were overwhelmed when your first starter kit showed up at the door. Start from that place when you speak. What would overwhelm you? What would encourage you? Write it below.

_____

_____

_____

_____

Tip 3: Go where the people are. No, literally go. I want you to close this workbook and book two classes in the next 30 days where you have friends. If that's an hour away, go. Check the boxes below when you have the dates confirmed. Even if only one person shows, it's worth the drive. That one person knows 2000 people!

☐ Class 1   ☐ Class 2

Tip 4: Speak with your friends that have large friend circles. You know what I'm going to have you do here! Write down the ten people you know with the largest sphere of influence. Then start building that relationship with them. Maybe the first ten conversations have nothing to do with oils, and that's ok. Start dropping seeds. If you get them on fire, what would that do for your business with them as a megaphone? Write their names below.

_____

_____

_____

_____

_____

_____

Tip 5: Say out loud, "My name is _____, and I am going to have a SIMPLE class tonight." That means no bells and whistles, no food, no folders, no fifty books on the table, no Cricut cutters. Keep it SIMPLE. Everything you do has to be copied! Don't scare away your leaders before they walk out the front door. They have to know they can do this, too. You get them to respond by not scaring them away with your actions.

CHAPTER 18

PERFECT PERSISTENCE: 7 TO 15 CONVERSATIONS

Do you text people the morning of the class to remind them? Do you remind them of why they are coming to the class, and how it will be tailored to them?

Do you build the relationship leading up to the class? Are you positive and encouraging, and offering a solution to their questions?

What do you do if they don't show up? What do you do if they say no to the first couple of classes?

Write your answer here: _____

_____

What is the gentle touch?

_____

_____

_____

_____

Write down an example of how you pour into someone solely for the sake of dropping seeds, until the moment is right and you can pursue them for your

team. _____

_____

_____

_____

The 7 to 15 Principle

Let's practice the 7 to 15 principle. For the next five people you talk to about oils, I want you to touch base, gently, 7 to 15 times. Some conversations may be oils related, and some may be seed planting without oils, and relationship building. When you get them to attend a class, write down how many conversations you had before that happened. With some people, it truly may only take one or two conversations. With others, like me, it may be the full seven or more. Track it so you can see the amount of labor you need to put in. Many times, we just give up way too early. The seed is in the ground, but you never watered it. Or it got watered and fertilized, but you walked away just as it was about to sprout, missing the one moment you'd been waiting for.

Let's track.

Person 1:

Conversations: ☐ ☐ ☐ ☐ ☐ ☐ ☐ ☐ ☐ ☐ ☐ ☐ ☐ ☐ ☐

How many conversations did it take for them to physically show up for a class? _____

Person 2:

Conversations: ☐ ☐ ☐ ☐ ☐ ☐ ☐ ☐ ☐ ☐ ☐ ☐ ☐ ☐ ☐

How many conversations did it take for them to physically show up for a class? _____

Person 3:

Conversations: ☐ ☐ ☐ ☐ ☐ ☐ ☐ ☐ ☐ ☐ ☐ ☐ ☐ ☐ ☐

How many conversations did it take for them to physically show up for a class? _____

Person 4:

Conversations: ☐ ☐ ☐ ☐ ☐ ☐ ☐ ☐ ☐ ☐ ☐ ☐ ☐ ☐ ☐

How many conversations did it take for them to physically show up for a class? _____

Person 5:

Conversations: ☐ ☐ ☐ ☐ ☐ ☐ ☐ ☐ ☐ ☐ ☐ ☐ ☐ ☐ ☐

How many conversations did it take for them to physically show up for a class? _____

- Half the battle is simply asking.

Who are the people in your circle, that if they signed on someone else's team, you'd cry? Write their names down below. Then pursue them first.

_____

_____

_____

CHAPTER 19

DIAMOND RISING DECKS: FOLLOW UP AT ITS BEST

Essential Rewards is the key to _____

Go into every class prepared for _____

Diamond Rising Deck Training

The Contact Me Card = A Prospecting Funnel

The Distributor Card = An Aromatherapy Funnel

The Diamond Rising Leader Card = A Business Training Funnel

8 in 10 people do not go inactive because of the cost of the oils. It is a

_____

_____

The Diamond Rising Decks are A funnel. What is your funnel? What system have you used? How many of your personally enrolled stay in Young Living? How many of your personally enrolled spend 300PV? Are they trained on the products?

Before you even have your card deck, I want you to do a little practice run of how a funnel works.

For your next three people you sign, take the time to do just a few things for them. This isn't even the full aromatherapy funnel. If it has been a while since you've signed someone, go back and do this with some of your previously enrolled and see what happens. We are going to call this a little investment exercise.

Person 1:

☐ Walk them through their kit.

☐ Hand them a pocket reference guide and show them how to use it.

☐ Immediately schedule 101, 102, 103 and 104 classes (get them on the calendar, preferably with some of their friend circles. Explain that if three people get kits, theirs is free).

☐ Generate a link for them with their number (as sponsor and enroller) so they can sign people when you are not around.

☐ Show them how to log into the Virtual Office and place an Essential Rewards order.

☐ Build a three month Essential Rewards wish list for them based off the information on their Contact Me card.

☐ Put *Fearless* and the *Fearless* calendar in their hands, or any tool you use to train the lifestyle, and incentivize them to read it and use their kit.

Date they got on ER: _____

What they spend in Month 1: _____ Month 2: _____

Month 3: _____

Person 2:

☐ Walk them through their kit.

☐ Hand them a pocket reference guide and show them how to use it.

☐ Immediately schedule 101, 102, 103 and 104 classes (get them on the calendar, preferably with some of their friend circles. Explain that if three people get kits, theirs is free).

☐ Generate a link for them with their number (as sponsor and enroller) so they can sign people when you are not around.

☐ Show them how to log into the Virtual Office and place an Essential Rewards order.

☐ Build a three month Essential Rewards wish list for them based off the information on their Contact Me card .

☐ Put *Fearless* and the *Fearless* calendar in their hands, or any tool you use to train the lifestyle, and incentivize them to read it and use their kit.

Date they got on ER: _____

What they spend in Month 1: _____ Month 2: _____

Month 3: _____

Person 3:

☐ Walk them through their kit.

☐ Hand them a pocket reference guide and show them how to use it.

☐ Immediately schedule 101, 102, 103 and 104 classes (get them on the calendar, preferably with some of their friend circles. Explain that if three people get kits, theirs is free).

☐ Generate a link for them with their number (as sponsor and enroller) so they can sign people when you are not around.

☐ Show them how to log into the Virtual Office and place an Essential Rewards order.

☐ Build a three month Essential Rewards wish list for them based off the information on their Contact Me card.

☐ Put *Fearless* and the *Fearless* calendar in their hands, or any tool you use to train the lifestyle, and incentivize them to read it and use their kit.

Date they got on ER: _____

What they spend in Month 1: _____ Month 2: _____

Month 3: _____

ER is what happens when you invest in people. Make the investment. Build the relationship, beyond the starter kit.

CHAPTER 20

METHODS OF TEACHING

One of my favorite lines of this chapter: *play until you find your gifts.*

How to Get *Unstuck*

Write down the five steps of how to use this book effectively. How do you pull yourself out of a stuck space?

Step 1:

_____

_____

_____

Step 2:

_____

_____

_____

Step 3:

_____

_____

_____

Step 4:

_____

_____

_____

Step 5:

_____

_____

_____

When you find something that works in network marketing, the secret to the rank is _____.

When Diamonds made rank, what were their stories?

1)_____

2)_____

3)_____

What happens when you stop doing the thing that got you the rank? _____

_____

When you are picking the type of class you want to teach, _____

_____

- *Look at what you've already done successfully, and that's your way. Go back to the method that got you your rank in the first place. No distractions.*
- *The months you don't teach, you are in a holding pattern.*
- *If you are frustrated with the pace you are growing, the secret is in your calendar. It's as easy as that.*
- *The people around you don't need a bracelet class to get cough relief. They need to know you have a solution to their problem. Be the solution finder, and you will have full classes... without plants, beads, pretty stickers, or cool titles.*

Give an honest assessment. Do you believe you've been putting time into your business in the ways required that will actually lead to OGV growth? Yes or no? _____

I'm going to give you permission to poke around this book, because I want you to start teaching right away, and not wait until the last page. Take a look at the 15 styles of classes and pick the top three you're interested in teaching. Skip to those chapters and read them first. Then, I want you to schedule a class with that style of sharing.

Check the classes that catch your attention most:

☐ Class 1: The In-Person Class

☐ Class 2: Purple Bags

☐ Class 3: Textable Classes

☐ Class 4: DVD Teaching: Playing the Role of the Hostess

☐ Class 5: Oils on the Body: The Personal Loan, Informal Sharing

☐ Class 6: Online Classes: Vimeo, Zoom, YouTube

☐ Class 7: Social Media Classes: Facebook and Instagram

☐ Class 8: Lunch and Learns, Sip and Sniff, Simple Swap, Ditch and Switch

☐ Class 9: Speed Oiling

☐ Class 10: Make and Takes that Work

☐ Class 11: Speaking At Events

☐ Class 12: Teacher Training Classes

☐ Class 13: Classes for Business Owners

☐ Class 14: Blogging and Vlogging

☐ Class 15: Vendor Events

I've hit you pretty hard with homework so far, so for this next section on the 15 types of classes, I'm going to lay off a bit. I just want you to do a solid self-evaluation of where your strengths lie by testing a few of these teaching methods. Remember, they all work! They all have results! No particular one is better than another! However, that doesn't mean they resonate with your gift set, so play. Play until you find the system that works for you, the system that can be copied by the thousands of leaders that will follow you.

For the next fifteen chapters, I'm only going to provide three short worksheets. I want you to test out three of the classes above, then fill out the worksheets to step back and verbally see how they went for you. I want you to give yourself a solid self-assessment. Then we'll jump back in right where we left off in the book.

How do you do this? Grab the 101, 102, 103, or 104 script from the back of this book. Pick one of the 15 methods and read through the chapter on it. Gather your supplies (less is more), and get out there and oil people up. Then write your results on the following pages.

WORKSHEET FOR DEMO CLASS 1
(covers Chapters 21-35)

Type of class: _____

Date I taught this class: _____

Oil I Put on Topically Before the Class: _____

Prep Required for the class: _____

_____

_____

Structure of my class: _____

_____

_____

Who came to the class: _____

_____

_____

Number of Contact Me cards collected: _____

Number of starter kit sales: _____

Number of people on Essential Rewards from this class: _____

Things that went well: _____

_____

_____

How I felt teaching this type of class: _____

_____

_____

What I could improve on: _____

_____

_____

What I can do to simplify what I did: _____

_____

_____

Can this class be copied by my leaders? _____

Why or why not? _____

_____

_____

Can I do this 4-6 times a month to rank up? _____

What is my weakness with this type of class? _____

_____

_____

_____

What are my strengths with this type of class? _____

_____

_____

_____

Is this type of class within my gift set? _____

_____

_____

Would I teach this class again? Why or why not? _____

_____

_____

_____

WORKSHEET FOR DEMO CLASS 2

Type of class: _____

Date I taught this class: _____

Oil I Put on Topically Before the Class: _____

Prep Required for the class: _____

_____

_____

Structure of my class: _____

_____

_____

Who came to the class: _____

_____

_____

Number of Contact Me cards collected: _____

Number of starter kit sales: _____

Number of people on Essential Rewards from this class: _____

Things that went well: _____

_____

_____

How I felt teaching this type of class: _____

_____

_____

What I could improve on: _____

_____

_____

What I can do to simplify what I did: _____

_____

_____

Can this class be copied by my leaders? _____

Why or why not? _____

_____

_____

Can I do this 4-6 times a month to rank up? _____

What is my weakness with this type of class? _____

_____

_____

_____

What are my strengths with this type of class? _____

_____

_____

_____

Is this type of class within my gift set? _____

_____

_____

Would I teach this class again? Why or why not? _____

_____

_____

_____

WORKSHEET FOR DEMO CLASS 3

Type of class: _____

Date I taught this class: _____

Oil I Put on Topically Before the Class: _____

Prep Required for the class: _____

_____

_____

Structure of my class: _____

_____

_____

Who came to the class: _____

_____

_____

Number of Contact Me cards collected: _____

Number of starter kit sales: _____

Number of people on Essential Rewards from this class: _____

Things that went well: _____

_____

_____

How I felt teaching this type of class: _____

_____

_____

What I could improve on: _____

_____

_____

What I can do to simplify what I did: _____

_____

_____

Can this class be copied by my leaders? _____

Why or why not? _____

_____

_____

Can I do this 4-6 times a month to rank up? _____

What is my weakness with this type of class? _____

_____

_____

_____

What are my strengths with this type of class? _____

_____

_____

_____

Is this type of class within my gift set? _____

_____

_____

Would I teach this class again? Why or why not? _____

_____

CHAPTER 36

THINGS THAT DON'T WORK

Make a list below of all the things that "don't work" when building your business. Then put a Star by the things you've done or have considered doing as part of "business operations." Circle them so you see them, and NEVER EVER do them.

What are seven blunders that I see happen EVERY DAY in Young Living?

I'll give you a hint. Do you know that I don't know a single Royal Crown Diamond who made rank by making oils shelves or homemade soap? I don't know any Royal Crown Diamonds who were wildly successful with a retail storefront, and built their business using the model of selling one oil at a time, and no starter kits. If that's the job description you're going for, why are you doing different actions?

Write down the 7 blunders below:

1)_____

2)_____

3)_____

4)_____

5)_____

6)_____

7)_____

You have everything you need to move forward. Don't second guess yourself. Just find humans and oil them.

CHAPTER 37

LEADING SENTENCES THAT START CONVERSATIONS

Do you see how close you are once the conversation has begun?

Don't use your personality as _____

Any skill can be learned if _____

Write down your top 3: "I can't do this" or "I'm not good at that", or "my personality type doesn't do that."

Then I want you to find a crayon and SCRIBBLE THE WORDS OUT WITH THE BLACKEST BLACK YOU CAN FIND SO YOU NEVER SEE THE WORDS AGAIN. You were made for more than excuses.

I can't.....

_____

_____

_____

How about this? "I can do ALL THINGS through Christ who strengthens me." Philippians 4:13.

Your decision to fight equals your level of success.

When I am approaching someone I don't know, I size them up. Do we have anything in common?

Write down a list of things about yourself. It may be what you do, how you parent, what you love, how you play, what you believe, or anything along those lines. Spell out YOU below.

Person 1, I connected by saying: _____

_____

_____

Person 2, I connected by saying:

_____

_____

Person 3, I connected by saying:

_____

_____

_____

CHAPTER 38

EXPANDING YOUR CIRCLE: HOW TO TAP INTO FRIENDS OF FRIENDS

Systematically _____

Sign your circle, then sign their circle.

Come up with your version of Jessica's text below.

Now, (you know what I'm going to say here). Send it to twenty random people on your team. Get them plugged in all over again to a 101, 102, 103 and 104 class. Use the Contact Me cards when you show up to teach to know what they need. Reignite their fire. Tell them you want to get ten people signed under them on ER so they don't have to pay for their oils, NingXia, or Thieves, but their Young Living check covers it. 10 people on ER at 300PV would mean a $240 dollar check. Getting ten people signed under one person may seem hard, but it's not really hard when you divide that over the Core 4 classes. That's two or three people in each class that sign up.

Then if you look at the multiplication factor, you now have ten more people with ten more friend circles that want their friends to hear about oils. There it goes, on and on and on. That's how you help your product users get their products for free, and never drop off Essential Rewards. You put them first.

Take that text you wrote at the start of this chapter, that's in your own words, and (right now) text it to twenty people on your team. Some may say, "yes". Some may say, "no". Some may say, "not right now." Even one "yes" is worth it, right? Especially if any of the ten you sign under them also take off.

Friends of friends is how I built my organization without knowing anyone.

Texting my team:

☐ ☐ ☐ ☐ ☐ ☐ ☐ ☐ ☐ ☐ ☐ ☐ ☐ ☐ ☐ ☐ ☐ ☐ ☐ ☐

When you get a "yes", set a date for a 101, 102, 103 or 104 class using your favorite teaching style from the previous chapters. Then funnel them to the next class in the Core 4. You have this!

6-month check in

(Fill this out six months after you initially opened this book). If you've been teaching to friends of friends, what is that doing to your OGV?

Plot your OGV below:

Month 1: _____

Month 2: _____

Month 3: _____

Month 4: _____

Month 5: _____

Month 6: _____

CHAPTER 39

HOW TO CRAFT YOUR PERSONAL STORY

Telling your story, I am convinced, is the most powerful part of your class. It's where your passion lies.

A good story has three critical components. What are they?

1)_____

2)_____

3)_____

Answer the following questions to start to craft your own personal story.

1) Who invited you to your first oils class?

_____

_____

_____

_____

_____

_____

_____

_____

_____

2) Why did you initially set foot in the door? What drew you there?

3) Did you get the kit right away?

4) If not, what got you to get it later?

5) What was your "wow" moment? Tell me why you oil.

6) Are there any other oils in the starter kit that got your attention?

7) Why do you believe in Young Living?

8) Was there a transformation for you?

9) What about a life lesson? Did you learn anything in the process?

10) What do you want that room of people to know about oils? Spill your passion.

Now I want you to take all that wonderful information you just jotted down, and get it condensed to under two minutes in a solid bulletpointed list that you can glance at and still speak from. Do that below.

Practice telling your story in the mirror ten times over a series of a few days. I'm going to ask you to do something incredibly uncomfortable (even news anchors hate doing this. We call it an "air check"). Record yourself.

If you're so uncomfortable doing that, at the least do a voice recording and not a video. Get yourself on tape and listen to it back. I also want you to watch the length of your story. You should be able to tell it in 3 to 5 minutes. If your one-hour oils class requires a 45-minute personal story, you're going to lose people.

Check the boxes below for each practice round of your story. Write down how long it took to tell it the first time; and then how long it took to tell it the tenth time.

Running time, personal story Take 1: _____

Running time, personal story Take 10: _____

Practice rounds:

☐ ☐ ☐ ☐ ☐ ☐ ☐ ☐ ☐ ☐

You are practiced-up!

Now go tell the world.

CHAPTER 40

ESSENTIAL REWARDS 101: ER WITHOUT THE SALES PITCH

Telling your story, I am convinced, is the most powerful part of your class. It's where your passion lies.

Essential Rewards is the only way you can _____ successfully.

You are saving your oiler the most money by offering Essential Rewards. Write down three points to consider:

_____

_____

_____

_____

You are not "salsey" when you train.

Are you transfer buying from yourself? How can you teach it if you're still buying things at the grocery store that are in the Virtual Office?

If you need a place to begin, start with *Fearless*.

At the end of my classes, I like to offer up a free *Fearless* book to attendees. I always ask, "was this a bit overwhelming? Are you unsure where to start? This tiny book walks you through, room by room, how to start swapping things out. Start where you are convicted. Accept the 10 *Fearless* challenges, and go room by room to kick chemicals to the curb." The charts at the end of *Fearless* run them through which Young Living products to swap out for the toxic products in their home, with item numbers on what to order.

I challenge you to do this yourself. Print the calendar. Accept the 10 challenges. Get your own diffuser going for a month. Use every oil in your starter kit over 11 days. Drink the NingXia and spray the Thieves. Watch the videos in the Getting Started tab. Sometimes we get so far removed from our own business, we forget what it felt like when our kit first showed up. That piece of mercy we had at the beginning, that understood the feelings of learning something new, has disappeared. For you to relate to your new oiler, you need to walk through it all over again, and speak with compassion.

Read *Fearless* again. Fill out your own *Fearless* calendar. Remember what it was like to learn to oil. Then, every time you speak, speak from that place of new discovery. Speak from that place of "one step at a time".

the Simple Swap

26 SECONDS
AFTER EXPOSURE, CHEMICALS ARE FOUND IN MEASURABLE AMOUNTS IN THE HUMAN BODY.

The National Institute of Occupational Safety and Health studied 2,983 ingredients in our products at home

884 toxic ingredients
314 caused biological mutations.
218 caused reproductive problems.
778 were toxic to the human body.
146 cause cancer tumors

Take it one room at a time!

Laundry
• laundry detergent
• fabric softener
• stain spray
• stain stick
• bleach

Beauty Care
• facewash
• toner
• moisturizer
• lotion
• eye cream
• makeup
• makeup remover
• deodorant
• brightener cream

Kitchen
• dishwasher detergent
• counter spray
• dish soap
• hand soap

Bathrooms
• shampoo
• conditioner
• facewash
• bodywash
• toothpaste
• dental floss
• mouthwash

Cleaning Closet
• dusting spray
• carpet cleaner
• toilet cleaner
• mirror/window spray
• floor cleaner
• air freshener
• cleaning wipes

Baby + Kids
• diaper rash cream
• baby oil
• baby wipes
• lotions
• vitamins
• kids shampoo
• kids body wash
• kids toothpaste
• enzymes

Supplements
• immunity
• daily vitamins
• brain and heart
• allergies
• probiotics
• hormones
• fish oil
• digestive issues

Etc.
• suncreen
• bug repellant spray
• cough drops
• pain cream
• energy boosters

the Simple Swap

TAKING IT ONE ROOM AT A TIME

BEAUTY CARE

Facewash • ART Gentle Cleanser		5361
Toner • ART Refreshing Toner		5360
Moisturizer • ART Light Moisturizer		5362
Eye cream • Wolfberry Eye Cream		5145
Brighterner cream • Sheerlume´		4833
Makeup • Savvy Minerals		varies
Deodorant • AromaGuard Deodorant		3752
Lotion • Hand & Body Lotion		5201
Makeup remover • YL Seedlings Baby Wipes		20428

LAUNDRY

Laundry detergent • Thieves Laundry Soap		5349
Fabric softener • (wool dryer balls + essential oils)		
Stain spray • Thieves Household CLeaner		3743
Stain stick • Thieves Household Cleaner		3743
Bleach • Thieves Household Cleaner		3743

BATHROOMS

Shampoo • Copaiba Vanilla Shampoo		5194121
Conditioner • Copaiba Vanilla Conditioner		5195121
Facewash • ART Gentle Cleanser		5361
Bodywash • Bath & Shower Gel-Sensation		3748
Toothpaste • Thieves AromaBright Toothpaste		3039
Dental floss • Thieves Dental Floss		4464122
Mouthwash • Thieves Fresh Essence Mouthwash		3683
Kids bathroom • see Baby + Kids		

KITCHEN

Dish soap • Thieves Dish Soap		5350
Hand soap • Thieves Foaming Hand Soap		3674
Dishwasher detergent • Thieves Dishwasher Powder		5762
Counter spray • Thieves Household Cleaner		3743

BABY + KIDS

Baby lotion • YL Seedlings Calm Scent		20438
Baby oil • YL Seedlings Calm Scent		20373
Baby wipes • YL Seedlings Calm Scent		20428
Diaper rash cream • YL Seedlings Diaper Rash Cream		20398
Kids shampoo • KidScents Shampoo		3686
Kids bodywash • KidScents Bath Gel		3684
Kids toothpaste • KidScents Slique Toothpaste		4574
Kids lotion • KidScents Lotion		3682
First Aid Kit • KidScents Oils		varies
(TummyGize, Owie, GeneYus, Sleepyize, SniffleEase)		
Diffusers for kids: Dolphin Reef Ultrasonic Diffuser		5333
Dino Land Ultrasonic Diffuser		5332

CLEANING CLOSET

Dusting • Thieves Household Cleaner		3743
Carpet cleaner • Thieves Household Cleaner		3743
Mirror/window spray • TThieves Household Cleaner		3743
Toilet cleaner • Thieves Household Cleaner		3743
Floor cleaner • Thieves Household Cleaner		3743
Air freshener • Desert Mist Diffuser		21558
Cleaning wipes • Thieves Wipes		3756

ETC.

Sunscreen • Mineral Sunscreen Lotion		20667
Deet bug repellant • Insect Repellant		20701
Cough drops • Thieves Infused Cough Drops		5670
Pain cream • Cool Azul Pain Cream Relief		5759
Energy boosters • Ningxia NITRO		3054

SUPPLEMENTS

Immune system • NingXia Red		3042
Daily vitamins • Master Formula		5292
Allergies • Allerzyme		3288
Brain/heart health • MindWise		4747
Probiotics • Life 9		18299
Hormone sypport • Progessence Plus Serum		4640
Fish oil • Omegagize		3097
Digestive support • Essentialzyme		3272

Now, I want you to make a list of every single item in the Virtual Office that is not an oil or a makeup product that you have not tried. Make it a point every single Essential Rewards order to try at least one new thing. How can you talk about the products when you've not used the products?

Pen your list below.

My Transfer Buying Wish List

#beasexcitedasUsha

_____ _____

_____ _____

_____ _____

_____ _____

Break your own list up by order of importance, and make your own three-month ER wish list.

Why am I having you do all this? Because this is how you train a new oiler. If you've put a reference guide in their hand, trained them on *Fearless* and the calendar, made a three-month ER wish list with them, gotten them into the Core 4 classes, and signed their circle so they have the income to afford the oils; you have taken away 95 percent of their excuses.

You are in the business of excuses destruction.

It takes time, relationships, and patience; but it builds an empire.

Now, let's talk about ER one last time. What are the eight action steps you can do to make your ER presentation seamless?

1)_____

2)_____

3)_____

4)_____

5)_____

6)_____

7)_____

8)_____

Write out a few lines you can say about ER (and practice them) to make it roll off your tongue when you get to that part of the presentation. Practice what you wrote.

CHAPTER 41

CLOSING IN A WAY THAT LEADS TO KIT SALES

Write down the 9 tips for a powerful close:

1)_____

2)_____

3)_____

4)_____

5)_____

6)_____

7)_____

8)_____

9)_____

What was your objection in getting your kit?

_____

_____

_____

_____

_____

_____

How would you talk yourself out of it, using Teri Secrest's technique?

_____

_____

_____

_____

_____

_____

Your close is the most uncomfortable part of the class, especially if sales are not your jam. Make it more comfortable by practicing. Either write your own close, end with passion with the end of the Core 4 Scripts, or practice the Bold Close scripts in the back of *Unstuck*. Cross each box off after you have practiced. Then go try a script and a close on your mom or best friend.

☐ ☐ ☐ ☐ ☐ ☐ ☐ ☐ ☐ ☐

If you have read this book and completed this workbook and are still having no-show classes, check off this checklist to do one final doubletake to make sure you've hit all your bases.

CHAPTER 42

THE GRASS IS GREENER ON THE OTHER SIDE SYNDROME

Run a no-drama team.

Don't rubberneck other people's journeys.

Only compare you to you.

Drop all expectations of what you think your leaders need to be doing.

Stop getting hurt when your prospects are signing elsewhere. Simply up your follow up game.

Still fearful of your business?

Write out the words of John 14:27 and Joshua 1:9:

_____

_____

_____

_____

_____

_____

What have been your "grass is greener on the other side" moments?

_____

_____

_____

_____

_____

_____

Why is the grass best right where you are?

_____

_____

_____

_____

_____

_____

_____

Be so busy looking forward at the next thing that you don't notice the negativity. Make your grass the greener grass.

CHAPTER 43

A SPIRIT OF CONTENTMENT

Why do you need to fight beyond the rank of Star or Senior Star?

_____

_____

_____

_____

_____

_____

_____

What was Steve's weakness in strategy?

_____

_____

_____

_____

_____

_____

_____

What was Rayquaza's weakness in strategy?

_____

_____

_____

_____

_____

_____

_____

What do 92 and 8 mean?

_____

_____

_____

_____

_____

_____

_____

This is the way Young Living suggests you structure your team.

Rising Star Method

STEP 3 { ⭐ 1K ⭐ 1K (500) (500)

STEP 2 { (500) (500)

STEP 1 { (300) (300) (300) (300) (300) (300) (300)

If you are not structured this way, what can you do to correct the strategy?

_____

_____

_____

_____

_____

_____

_____

Do you have a spirit of contentment? What is your weakness?

_____

_____

_____

_____

_____

_____

_____

Write out your own prayer of surrender. Ask the Lord for the strength to fight. Pray this every time you feel lost. You are WORTHY.

CHAPTER 44

THE CURSE OF EXPECTATIONS

What does a REAL Young Living business look like? Write out 10 truths of a Young Living business. Put a star next to things you **used** to believe.

1)_____

2)_____

3)_____

4)_____

5)_____

6)_____

7)_____

8)_____

9)_____

10)_____

What makes this job unusual? List five things. Add a few of your own ideas to the list as to why YOU think this is the best job in the world for you.

1)_____

2)_____

3)_____

4)_____

5)_____

What is your WHY? What keeps you going?

How do you plan to get there?

_____

_____

_____

_____

_____

_____

_____

_____

_____

_____

_____

_____

Having a goal is smart. Putting a timeline on that goal and telling your-self you're not good at this if you don't hit the deadline could cost you your business.

CHAPTER 45

RINSE AND REPEAT TO DIAMOND

THE STORY OF KATHY: 12,000 TO 19,000 OGV IN 12 WEEKS

How did Sarah lose Diamond?

_____

_____

_____

_____

_____

_____

_____

_____

Do what got you _____

If your OGV is completely stuck, consider the following things, check them off before you say, "I have tried it all!"

☐ Does your OGV increase every month, or are you in a holding pattern, maintaining but not reaching new people?

☐ Do you check to see how many enrollers you have each month in the Oily Tools app? Doubling that number (the number of people that sign people up) is the fastest way to rank. Work with your runners.

☐ When was the last time you sold a kit? Are you expecting your leaders to do things you are not doing?

☐ Have you picked a method of sharing that has results?

☐ Do you have an idea of what your gifts and talents are, and what you need to do to do this?

☐ If you've never sold a kit before, is there a certain type of class that resonates with you? Have you gotten out there, listened to the needs of people, then been assertive enough (7 to 15 conversations) before you walk away?

☐ If you are already a Star, Senior Star, or above, and you built your team, what did you do to build it? Since you became stagnant, have you done the same actions that initially led to your first rank up?

☐ How BAD do you want this? Are you willing to do things that make you uncomfortable, until they become more comfortable? Are you willing to speak, even if it may mean the way you're perceived is not favorable; because their health matters more to you than their opinion of you?

There is never an end to the cycle of crazy until you step outside your comfort zone. Freedom is after the fight.

Where are you placing your time? Is it in direct income-producing activities, or other activities?

Write out what you've spent your time on in the past two weeks for your business, then guess the amount of time you spent on it. We're going to plot it out on a pie chart so you have a visualization of what your business actions look like.

Honest Self-Evaluation

Now, I want you to look at the activities you're doing, and put them into certain categories:

- ☐ Teaching classes.

- ☐ Training the lifestyle with solid follow up.

- ☐ Building the relationships.

- ☐ Prep for classes (marketing, supplies, practicing).

- ☐ Training your leaders.

- ☐ Anything outside this short list (that is not related to one of the items above).

Figure out what percentages you're spending on each category. About 75-80 percent of your time must be in teaching and prospecting, or you will not see steady OGV growth in your business. Plot out what you see below in different colors by category. (I've given you permission to color in this workbook TWICE!)

You've already handed what you were holding back to the Lord. You've already let the outcome go. Now you move. Do this one brick at a time, one class at a time, once investment in a life at a time.

You are unstuck.

CHAPTER 46

CLOSING OUT WITH HOPE

What is your hope story?

Where are you RIGHT now?

Where do you need release?

I want you to write the end of your own story exactly the way you see it in your head. Bring that big 'ole dream board out and use those pictures to fill this page with words. Write out what you see happening when you do this thing: when you're teaching a class a week, when you train ER and train your leaders, and when you WALK for Silver, Gold, Platinum and Diamond.

What happens to your family?

Tell your story below. Then you read that story every single time you let that thought enter your head that you can't do this. You read it over and over again. You take your story WITH YOU on stage when you go get that big trophy from corporate for hitting rank. You wear your story with pride. Then use it to inspire tens of thousands who are where you are right now.

Your story was meant to be shared, hope-bringer. Those dark places you're at will not last forever. They will become the cement someone else needs under their feet to pull them from despair.

Write it down.

WALK THE WORDS.

CHAPTER 47

BONUS CHAPTER FOR THE UNSTUCK WORKBOOK

ACTING OUT YOUR DREAMS

You now know how to talk to total strangers.

You know how to open conversations.

You know how to follow up.

You know how to teach like a boss; and you have more than a dozen ideas to try when you feel your momentum is slowing down.

You know how to ignite your mojo, and move again.

You know how to banish bad thoughts from your head, and work out the positive.

You have realistic expectations.

You know what hustle looks like.

You have goals in your head.

You have worked out your dreams.

Let's put action to the next step in *Unstuck*: teaching classes, getting people on Essential Rewards, and training your leaders.

What if, for 52 weeks. You taught one class a week, ran the Diamond Rising Deck funnel with your whole team, made sure every member had the Core 4 and ER wishlists, and knew how to look things up; and you ran *Gameplan*, *Ignite*, or *Unstuck* bootcamps a couple times a year with your team?

What would happen?

Those are the three powerhouse Income Producing Activities.

You have a system. You have a plan. It's time to put motion to it. I'm going to issue the *Unstuck* Challenge! Cross off a box a week every single time you hit a goal of teaching a class, every time you get your leaders on ER through solid aromatherapy training and your love of Young Living products, and run leadership training. Every time you coach a leader, write it down. Sketch your journey. Fill out the certificate at the end of *Unstuck* when you finish the book, workbook and bootcamp... That's step one. Then implement everything you have learned, and duplicate with your new leaders that say they can't get anyone to come to a class. You KNOW what to do. You KNOW how to get out. You know that a state of stuck is always rooted in fear. Freedom is on the other side of fear.

Once you have the chart below filled out with all 3 IPA's for 52 weeks (do SOMETHING for your leaders weekly; whether it's a coaching, live training, or full on bootcamp) Connect with SOMEONE (on your team or off your team) weekly. Then, you can check the boxes.

If you complete all 52 boxes, you're an *Unstuck* Super Diamond. Write me at oilabilitywithsarah@gmail.com after the 52 weeks are up, and I'll get something special in the mail to you just for making it a full year.

Track your starting OGV here: _____

Track your ending OGV here: _____

THE UNSTUCK CHALLENGE

Week 1 ☐ Taught a class ☐ ☐ ☐ ☐ Connected with a human ☐ trained a leader

Week 2 ☐ Taught a class ☐ ☐ ☐ ☐ Connected with a human ☐ trained a leader

Week 3 ☐ Taught a class ☐ ☐ ☐ ☐ Connected with a human ☐ trained a leader

Week 4 ☐ Taught a class ☐ ☐ ☐ ☐ Connected with a human ☐ trained a leader

Week 5 ☐ Taught a class ☐ ☐ ☐ ☐ Connected with a human ☐ trained a leader

Week 6 ☐ Taught a class ☐ ☐ ☐ ☐ Connected with a human ☐ trained a leader

Week 7 ☐ Taught a class ☐ ☐ ☐ ☐ Connected with a human ☐ trained a leader

Week 8 ☐ Taught a class ☐ ☐ ☐ ☐ Connected with a human ☐ trained a leader

Week 9 ☐ Taught a class ☐ ☐ ☐ ☐ Connected with a human ☐ trained a leader

Week 10 ☐ Taught a class ☐ ☐ ☐ ☐ Connected with a human ☐ trained a leader

Week 11 ☐ Taught a class ☐ ☐ ☐ ☐ Connected with a human ☐ trained a leader

Week 12 ☐ Taught a class ☐ ☐ ☐ ☐ ☐ Connected with a human ☐ trained a leader

Week 13 ☐ Taught a class ☐ ☐ ☐ ☐ ☐ Connected with a human ☐ trained a leader

Week 14 ☐ Taught a class ☐ ☐ ☐ ☐ ☐ Connected with a human ☐ trained a leader

Week 15 ☐ Taught a class ☐ ☐ ☐ ☐ ☐ Connected with a human ☐ trained a leader

Week 16 ☐ Taught a class ☐ ☐ ☐ ☐ ☐ Connected with a human ☐ trained a leader

Week 17 ☐ Taught a class ☐ ☐ ☐ ☐ ☐ Connected with a human ☐ trained a leader

Week 18 ☐ Taught a class ☐ ☐ ☐ ☐ ☐ Connected with a human ☐ trained a leader

Week 19 ☐ Taught a class ☐ ☐ ☐ ☐ ☐ Connected with a human ☐ trained a leader

Week 20 ☐ Taught a class ☐ ☐ ☐ ☐ ☐ Connected with a human ☐ trained a leader

Week 21 ☐ Taught a class ☐ ☐ ☐ ☐ ☐ Connected with a human ☐ trained a leader

Week 22 ☐ Taught a class ☐ ☐ ☐ ☐ ☐ Connected with a human ☐ trained a leader

Week 23 ☐ Taught a class ☐ ☐ ☐ ☐ ☐ Connected with a human ☐ trained a leader

Week 24 ☐ Taught a class ☐ ☐ ☐ ☐ ☐ Connected with a human ☐ trained a leader

Week 25 ☐ Taught a class ☐ ☐ ☐ ☐ ☐ Connected with a human ☐ trained a leader

Week 26 ☐ Taught a class ☐ ☐ ☐ ☐ ☐ Connected with a human ☐ trained a leader

Week 27 ☐ Taught a class ☐ ☐ ☐ ☐ ☐ Connected with a human ☐ trained a leader

Week 28 ☐ Taught a class ☐ ☐ ☐ ☐ ☐ Connected with a human ☐ trained a leader

Week 29 ☐ Taught a class ☐ ☐ ☐ ☐ ☐ Connected with a human ☐ trained a leader

Week 30 ☐ Taught a class ☐ ☐ ☐ ☐ ☐ Connected with a human ☐ trained a leader

Week 31 ☐ Taught a class ☐ ☐ ☐ ☐ ☐ Connected with a human ☐ trained a leader

Week 32 ☐ Taught a class ☐ ☐ ☐ ☐ ☐ Connected with a human ☐ trained a leader

Week 33 ☐ Taught a class ☐ ☐ ☐ ☐ ☐ Connected with a human ☐ trained a leader

Week 34 ☐ Taught a class ☐ ☐ ☐ ☐ ☐ Connected with a human ☐ trained a leader

Week 35 ☐ Taught a class ☐ ☐ ☐ ☐ ☐ Connected with a human ☐ trained a leader

Week 36 ☐ Taught a class ☐ ☐ ☐ ☐ ☐ Connected with a human ☐ trained a leader

Week 37 ☐ Taught a class ☐ ☐ ☐ ☐ ☐ Connected with a human ☐ trained a leader

Week 38 ☐ Taught a class ☐ ☐ ☐ ☐ ☐ Connected with a human ☐ trained a leader

Week 39 ☐ Taught a class ☐ ☐ ☐ ☐ ☐ Connected with a human ☐ trained a leader

Week 40 ☐ Taught a class ☐ ☐ ☐ ☐ ☐ Connected with a human ☐ trained a leader

Week 41 ☐ Taught a class ☐ ☐ ☐ ☐ ☐ Connected with a human ☐ trained a leader

Week 42 ☐ Taught a class ☐ ☐ ☐ ☐ ☐ Connected with a human ☐ trained a leader

Week 43 ☐ Taught a class ☐ ☐ ☐ ☐ ☐ Connected with a human ☐ trained a leader

Week 44 ☐ Taught a class ☐ ☐ ☐ ☐ ☐ Connected with a human ☐ trained a leader

Week 45 ☐ Taught a class ☐ ☐ ☐ ☐ ☐ Connected with a human ☐ trained a leader

Week 46 ☐ Taught a class ☐ ☐ ☐ ☐ ☐ Connected with a human ☐ trained a leader

Week 47 ☐ Taught a class ☐ ☐ ☐ ☐ ☐ Connected with a human ☐ trained a leader

Week 48 ☐ Taught a class ☐ ☐ ☐ ☐ ☐ Connected with a human ☐ trained a leader

Week 49 ☐ Taught a class ☐ ☐ ☐ ☐ ☐ Connected with a human ☐ trained a leader

Week 50 ☐ Taught a class ☐ ☐ ☐ ☐ ☐ Connected with a human ☐ trained a leader

Week 51 ☐ Taught a class ☐ ☐ ☐ ☐ ☐ Connected with a human ☐ trained a leader

Week 52 ☐ Taught a class ☐ ☐ ☐ ☐ ☐ Connected with a human ☐ trained a leader

The message is always about meeting the need.

#doitforgary

#oilsineveryhomeintheworld

BONUS COACHING SESSION FOR THE UNSTUCK WORKBOOK

This last section is for you to physically map out your personal road. How many classes are you away from your next rank? Do you see how close you are? Have you tracked your own personal statistics, so you know your weaknesses? Coach yourself, then you'll see how to coach your own team. Fill out each of the sheets after this page for yourself, then check in with yourself every three months, as you would a budding leader. Run yourself through all the funnels on each of the three cards on the Diamond Rising Deck. Remember, the more you PLAY with your oils, the more stories you will have. Never stop collecting stories!

Still can't find people? To recap, these are the places I told you to start looking:

12 QUICK TIPS FROM UNSTUCK

1. Go through your cell phone list and make contact without mentioning oils.

2. Accept the Starbucks/Panera challenge. Start up random conversations and collect contact information.

3. Sign your personal circle, your warm market.

4. Go through all the O's on your team and train on the Core 4 classes.

5. Hand out purple bags! Carry five at all times! (Mojo method).

6. Sign up for a vendor event and go with a flip kit and Contact Me cards. (Mojo method).

7. Sign friends of friends on your team. (A FAST way to rank when you know no one!)

8. Send textable classes.

9. Has EVERYONE on your team had the Core 4? Go through your whole team and systematically befriend them.

10. When was the last time you taught? Set the example for your team!

11. Open the Door and Talk to Humans Challenge. Talk to the gas station guy, neighbors in subdivision, post office, church, and cubicles. Speak to several people a week.

12. Accept the *Unstuck* challenge: Give this business one year of your life. Hold 52 classes. Love on humans. Run *Gameplan* or *Ignite* bootcamps, or *Unstuck* bootcamps a couple times yearly to fire up your leaders. Do *Fearless* mailings + the *Fearless* calendar to all your O's. Track your OGV! You HAVE this. You know who you are, and you know your fight is enough.

Now go get *Unstuck*.

UNSTUCK TWO-PAGE
Teacher Training

Intro to Teacher Training

Ninety-five percent of what I do is action. That is how you get to Diamond: it's not by thinking about what you're going to do, but by doing it. The tighter you keep your classes, the tighter you keep your teacher trainings, the tighter your advanced coaching, the easier you can be copied. I have consolidated the Teacher Training into two pages (or one page printed back to back), because that's how I train a new leader without giving them information overload. Most of the training is done in photos, so you're capturing your visual learners, too. Run through the Income Disclosure Guide, give the why, explain the comp plan in five minutes or less, show them the four things they must do to get a higher paycheck with the Rank Qualification graphic, show them how to log in and place their Essential Rewards order (and find the Rank Qualification and My Organization buttons), and give them their first homework assignment. Then set a date to meet again.

These final sheets in this section are coaching sheets. The Teacher Training pages are your very first business training. The coaching sheets are for following up with advanced leaders. I usually only use two sheets when I coach: rank mapping (to plot out how far they are from their next rank) and the Coaching Sheet (where I map out action steps to help them achieve the goals laid out on the Rank Mapping Sheets). If you have them track their stats as well (they take that sheet with them), when you meet again you can identify weaknesses. A dropping ER percentage rate means their leaders aren't training the lifestyle. A dip in the number of Stars or Senior Stars means there's not enough Teacher Training and Coaching going on. A dip in the number of new members means the leaders aren't teaching classes. For the coaching sheets, I print two sets. As we work through it, we both write down the numbers. One set goes home with me in my leader binder, the second set goes home with them to work on. We meet again in 3 months and see how close they've gotten to their goals.

The great thing is that these are FREE RESOURCES. You don't need to copy them out of this book. You can print them directly off my website, over and over again, at no cost. Go to oilabilityteam.com/unstuck and look for the coaching resources section. May this bless you as you train your leaders!

❶ Let's talk compensation!

This is what
#diamondrising
looks like

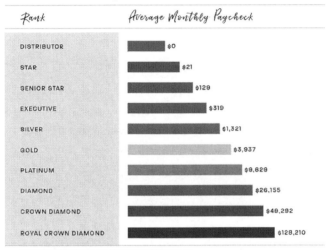

YOUNG LIVING *Ranks* AVERAGE MONTHLY INCOME

Rank — *Average Monthly Paycheck*

Rank	Average Monthly Paycheck
DISTRIBUTOR	$0
STAR	$21
SENIOR STAR	$129
EXECUTIVE	$319
SILVER	$1,321
GOLD	$3,937
PLATINUM	$9,829
DIAMOND	$26,155
CROWN DIAMOND	$49,292
ROYAL CROWN DIAMOND	$128,210

View the full 2018 Income Disclosure statement at:
https://static.youngliving.com/en-US/PDFS/IDSOnlineVersion_PDF_US.pdf

❷ Why Do A Young Living Business?

- No income ceiling.
- You're your own boss and set your own hours.
- Take time off and still get paid (residual income) .
- Oils are easier to share than a pan, clothing, or makeup because they are consumable.
- See the people around you experience financial freedom as they teach.
- Build time economy.
- Build relationships with those that love natural health.
- It doesn't matter how many people you know.
- You don't have to be good at speaking (or know a lot of people) because there are Many ways to build.
- Willable income.

❸ Young Living Compensation Plan (Let's break the check down!)

You're paid four ways:

1. Starter Kit bonuses ($50 per kit; $25 for the Starter Kit bonus and $25 for Fast Start).

2. Fast Start (25 percent on everything they order after the starter kit; only for 3 months).

3. Unilevel (8% on your level 1's, 5% on your level 2's, 4% on your level 3's, 4's, 5's).

4. Rising Star or Generation Leadership Bonuses (bonuses for strategizing your rank a certain way or for raising leaders once you hit the rank of Silver). For the purposes of

just starting the business, keep your strategy simple. Everyone goes under you as a Level 1 until you have ten people on Essential Rewards.

❹ Rank Qualification chart from the Virtual Office (Simple Strategy Coaching)

This is how you rank up! The nine ranks in Young Living are across the top. The four rows represent four things you need to do to hit the next rank: spend 100 PV, hit a certain volume (OGV), build your legs, and sustain 1000 PGV outside your legs. There are 9 ranks in Young Living: Star, Senior Star, Executive, Silver, Gold, Platinum, Diamond, Crown Diamond and Royal Crown Diamond. There are four things you must do to rank: 1) Spend 100PV. 2) Hit a certain OGV (volume) for each rank. That resets the 1st of every month (unless you get your people on Essential Rewards!) 3) Build legs. A leg is a person and a team under them. 4) Have PGV, or volume outside your legs. The four requirements are broken down below.

❺ Log in and do a quick tour of the Virtual Office so you understand how to place an ER order. Your order as a business builder must be 100pv to get your full paycheck. As a builder, being on Essential Rewards is good financial stewardship. To spend the $100 to get your full check, you're actually spending $90 because of Rewards Points. To pick out what you'd like, go over the reference guide and the YL catalogue side by side and build an ER wish list!

❻ Homework 1: Teach your first class + read two books: "Your Gameplan: Build A Life Beyond Survival Mode" and "The Essential Gameplan: Ignite Your Business In 2 Hours" before our next coaching session. Next time, we will cover *Fearless*, the *Fearless* 30-day calendar, and the Diamond Rising Deck for follow up training. You can do this!

This is my cell phone number if you have questions: _____

Print this sheet for free at oilabilityteam.com/unstuck to track your leader coaching!

UNSTUCK #DIAMONDRISING LEADER
Coaching Sheets

Gameplanner Rank-Mapping Sheet

Name _____ Distributor # _____ Date _____

Last six month's OGV

1 _____ 2 _____ 3 _____ 4 _____ 5 _____ 6 _____

Set OGV goals.

Current OGV _____ OGV Goal _____ OGV Needed _____

	current	goal	need	break it down
• Leg 1				
• Leg 2				
• Leg 3				
• Leg 4				
• Leg 5				
• Leg 6	ex: 1500	2000	500	5 kits / 2 classes
3 Month OGV targets				

Schedule 4-6 classes this month.

Dates of classes:

_____

_____

_____

Raise leaders.

Based on your rank mapping sheet, make a list of all the leaders in the last 6-12 months that have sold a kit on your weakest leg. Put down their names. Those are the people you work with, coach, and teach classes with and for this month. Work in your weakest places when you are fighting for a rank up.

_____

_____

_____

When you fill these sheets out, print two copies and work on them side by side. Both of you keep a copy until you check in again three months later.

Print these for free at oilabilityteam.com/unstuck.

UNSTUCK #DIAMONDRISING LEADER
Coaching Sheets

Coaching + Action Steps

Name_____ Distributor #_____ Date_____

Every 3-6 months, sit down for a 30-minute coaching session and revisit their goals, do rank mapping and stat tracking from the Gameplanner and work on their weak areas.

Do they need coaching on: ☐connecting with cold market ☐closing their classes ☐ meeting needs of people ☐doing strong follow up ☐teaching 1-2 classes a week (consistency) ☐ training their leaders ☐excuses ☐doing non income-producing activities (distraction) ☐ making sure each person on their team has the Core 4 classes ☐ tapping into friends of friends to build their team

Dates I coached this leader: _____

Action steps with 10 lines for notes and suggestions.

_____

_____

_____

_____

_____

_____

_____

_____

_____

_____

• Leg 1 _____

• Leg 2 _____

• Leg 3 _____

• Leg 4 _____

• Leg 5 _____

• Leg 6 _____

Print these for free at oilabilityteam.com/unstuck.

UNSTUCK #DIAMONDRISING LEADER
Coaching Sheets
Stat Tracking Homework

Track your statistics from the data on the Young Living Oil Tools app!

January
Rank:_____
Paycheck:_____
OGV:_____
Team size:_____
New members:_____
Going inactive:_____
Pace OGV on Day 1:_____
Projected OGV on Day 1:_____
Super recruiters:_____
Total ER:_____
Member % ER:_____
Enrollers:_____
Stars:_____
Senior Stars:_____
Executives:_____
Silvers:_____
Golds:_____
Platinums:_____

Februray
Rank:_____
Paycheck:_____
OGV:_____
Team size:_____
New members:_____
Going inactive:_____
Pace OGV on Day 1:_____
Projected OGV on Day 1:_____
Super recruiters:_____
Total ER:_____
Member % ER:_____
Enrollers:_____
Stars:_____
Senior Stars:_____
Executives:_____
Silvers:_____
Golds:_____
Platinums:_____

March
Rank:_____
Paycheck:_____
OGV:_____
Team size:_____
New members:_____
Going inactive:_____
Pace OGV on Day 1:_____
Projected OGV on Day 1:_____
Super recruiters:_____
Total ER:_____
Member % ER:_____
Enrollers:_____
Stars:_____
Senior Stars:_____
Executives:_____
Silvers:_____
Golds:_____
Platinums:_____

April
Rank:_____
Paycheck:_____
OGV:_____
Team size:_____
New members:_____
Going inactive:_____
Pace OGV on Day 1:_____
Projected OGV on Day 1:_____
Super recruiters:_____
Total ER:_____
Member % ER:_____
Enrollers:_____
Stars:_____
Senior Stars:_____
Executives:_____
Silvers:_____
Golds:_____
Platinums:_____

May
Rank:_____
Paycheck:_____
OGV:_____
Team size:_____
New members:_____
Going inactive:_____
Pace OGV on Day 1:_____
Projected OGV on Day 1:_____
Super recruiters:_____
Total ER:_____
Member % ER:_____
Enrollers:_____
Stars:_____
Senior Stars:_____
Executives:_____
Silvers:_____
Golds:_____
Platinums:_____

June
Rank:_____
Paycheck:_____
OGV:_____
Team size:_____
New members:_____
Going inactive:_____
Pace OGV on Day 1:_____
Projected OGV on Day 1:_____
Super recruiters:_____
Total ER:_____
Member % ER:_____
Enrollers:_____
Stars:_____
Senior Stars:_____
Executives:_____
Silvers:_____
Golds:_____
Platinums:_____

July
Rank:_____
Paycheck:_____
OGV:_____
Team size:_____
New members:_____
Going inactive:_____
Pace OGV on Day 1:_____
Projected OGV on Day 1:_____
Super recruiters:_____
Total ER:_____
Member % ER:_____
Enrollers:_____
Stars:_____
Senior Stars:_____
Executives:_____
Silvers:_____
Golds:_____
Platinums:_____

August
Rank:_____
Paycheck:_____
OGV:_____
Team size:_____
New members:_____
Going inactive:_____
Pace OGV on Day 1:_____
Projected OGV on Day 1:_____
Super recruiters:_____
Total ER:_____
Member % ER:_____
Enrollers:_____
Stars:_____
Senior Stars:_____
Executives:_____
Silvers:_____
Golds:_____
Platinums:_____

Weakness:_____   Action Steps:_____

Print these for free at oilabilityteam.com/unstuck.

GAMEPLAN RESOURCES
THAT WILL EXPLODE YOUR BUSINESS

To rank, stay focused on the only three things that directly grow your business:

- **Hold classes** • **Follow up** *and get people on Essential Rewards*
- **Train your leaders using Gameplan**

Hold Classes

Essential Oils 101 Audio CD

This is a 45 minute class on audio cd, recorded in a professional studio. The who, where, when, what, why of oils. Sarah uses these in her purple bags as a "class in a bag" to hand to complete strangers… and friends.

Toxin Free Life Audio CD

This is a 30 minute class on the Thieves line on audio cd, recorded in a professional studio. This targets cleaning supplies and toxins in the home. It's designed for those who aren't ready to jump in with oils yet, but really like the concept of a toxin free life.

FREE RESOURCES

The textable 101 audio class and Toxin Free life classes, the online Beauty School, and the 101 powerpoint at oilabilityteam.com! Look under "Share".

Follow Up

Fearless

This little book is a powerhouse, and the first of its kind in all of Young Living. For the majority of the people you share oils with, this is their first exposure to natural health. They are overwhelmed. This book is a systematic step-by-step oils explosion to get your new oiler emptying their bottles with courage. It trains the toxin-free lifestyle. It's the first book that should go out to every new kit holder.

Diamond Rising Decks

Are a full-on follow up system. You've had tools for your new oiler—this tool is for YOU. It takes the FEAR out of follow up for the very first time. The average person needs to be approached 7 to 15 times before they will commit to the

lifestyle. This gives you specific steps, tools, and concise training so you know exactly what comes next in each of those conversations, and it's never awkward for you. You simply stick to the system. Contact Me cards are for prospects. You'll learn their biggest health struggles, what areas of aromatherapy they want to learn more about, if they're already in Young Living, and how to best contact them. The Distributor cards are for people who have joined your team—and they're run through a powerful aromatherapy funnel that will drive them to research, label read, and take control of their own health. The Diamond Rising Leader cards take your budding leaders through an entire business funnel, step by step, from the starter kit all the way to Royal Crown Diamond. You track their entire Young Living journey on a series of three 4x6 cards, with simple checkmarks and minutes a day. It's a powerful and duplicatable system that works.

oilabilityteam.com

Train Your Leaders

Gameplan Book

The first duplicatable affordable training system in all of Young Living in the form of a book. This series went to number 1 on Amazon's entrepreneur catagory and sold over 700-thousand copies. How do you train your leaders? Use the book, workbook, and the free bootcamp at oilabilityteam.com. 25 chapters in the book, 25 worksheets, 12 free videos averaging 30 minutes each. Take it at your pace, pull two leaders through it, and rinse and repeat your way to Diamond. The system has worked for thousands upon thousands of Young Living distributors.

Gameplan Workbook

This is a critical part of the training system. It customizes the Gameplan book for you. This puts action to the things you read in the book and gets you to move.

Your Gameplan (the mini)

This is the first digestible prospecting book in all of Young Living. This book does the talking on the business for you. It covers the eight perks to a Young Living business, the Income Disclosure guide, and gets your prospect stacking up their job against a Young Living home based business.

Unstuck

Is the 2ND BOOK IN THE GAMEPLAN TRILOGY! Sarah collected thousands of responses and categorized them into 15 types of classes that have results. She lists four tried-and-true mojo methods to pull you out of a rut. There's 100 pages of Young Living specific mindset training, coaching to craft your personal story, how to lead with Essential Rewards in a compelling way that trains the lifestyle, training to set up an aromatherapy and business funnel that makes it comfortable to have multiple conversations to get your new oiler on ER. There are four scripts for the four starter kits—including a powerful NingXia script and a new Savvy Makeup script. She's collected dozens of leading sentences, tips for opening conversations with cold and warm market leads, and suggestions for following up. If your struggle is finding and connecting with humans, this will be the catapult your business has been waiting for.

Unstuck Workbook

Pairs perfectly with the Unstuck book. Unstuck gives you the knowledge and tools. The workbook tailors that knowledge directly to your needs and custom fits your experiences to the book to make it come alive for you. You'll find practical, tangible homework assignments inside that drive your business forward and pull you from a place of fear. It's not to be skipped! This is your personal Unstuck accountability system!

Ignite

Is a cliff-notes version of the full Gameplan book. This concise book is designed for your leaders that are not "all in" yet; those that are whetting their appetites with Young Living or are overwhelmed by a large book. Beta tested on dozens of blue personalities, the average read time for this book is 42 minutes. Yet it hits all the important topics that a new builder needs to know from the get-go: ER, the Virtual Office, the compensation plan, simple strategy, how you are paid, and the power and importance of consistently teaching. It ends with two scripts and a challenge to teach their first class to a family member or friend that night. If your leaders have clocked out or have stopped doing the things that got them to their rank in the first place—or if they're new and you have a blank slate, Ignite is the perfect tool.

The
Unstuck

20 Day Bootcamp Kicks off
Monday, January 6th!

170,000 oilers
went through Gameplan Bootcamp

Be part of the revolution at
the Oil Ability with Sarah Facebook page
at 8:30pm eastern!
Sarah will coach you through the
entire book in short sessions!

Fire up your team-- it's time to get Unstuck!

D. Gary Young

FATHER OF THE MODERN-DAY
ESSENTIAL OIL MOVEMENT.

—— 1949 - 2018 ——

Made in the USA
Middletown, DE
02 January 2020